LETTERS TO KATE

JUDY ROBLIN

Letters to Kate

ST PAULS

ST PAULS Publishing
187 Battersea Bridge Road, London SW11 3AS, UK
www.stpauls.ie

ISBN 085439 723 X

Set by TuKan DTP, Stubbington, Fareham, UK
Printed in Malta by Progress Press Company Limited

ST PAULS is an activity of the priests and brothers
of the Society of St Paul who proclaim the Gospel
through the media of social communication

In loving memory of a dear friend
Dom Alan Rees OSB

My thanks go to
Sr Veronica Ann (Tymawr)
and
Sr Dolores (Caldey Island)
who taught me how to write letters

and to
Benedicta
for collaboration and
encouragement at every stage

Foreword

Reading *Letters to Kate* is a real experience in itself. The author takes you into the heart of a cordial and loving relationship in which the older woman coaxes and accompanies the journey of the younger one who in her turn is able to deepen the commitment of the other.

At first sight these writings may come across as 'easy reading' about the spiritual life, but very soon that impression gives way to an awareness of someone who is already deeply immersed in the life of the Spirit. What I mean is that this book shows the whole spectrum of the spiritual life that is truly integrated into the day-to-day living. Although it is a little book, it has all the ingredients and the important crossroads you meet in the life that yearns to be lived to God.

Judy Roblin has that rare gift of bringing the wisdom of the Fathers and the Mothers (Benedict, Julian of Norwich, Nelson Mandela) fully alive and making it tangible for the people of today. This can only be achieved through the experience of meeting the sacred in ordinary people because she allowed the sacred love of God to touch upon her own heart.

The letters and certainly the poetry evoke spontaneously the yearnings of everyone's heart. It is no exaggeration to say that the comfort that came to me through these pages was deeply moving, not only emotionally but in my every layer: body, mind, soul and spirit – 'warts and all'!

I have no doubt that this great 'little book' will touch the lives of many.

Fr Daniel van Santvoort OCSO
Abbot of Caldey

Preface

It often seems that the Holy Spirit is more active in our lives at some times than others. In fact the Spirit is always at work; we just don't always realise it, or at least not until much later. It may be many years before some life-event brings the past to mind and we see our story in a new light. It is then that the saying rings true: life must be lived forwards but can only be understood backwards.

This became clear to me when in mid-life, during the process of moving house, I discovered a batch of letters written to me by my godmother Ailsa, for the most part during my university years. These letters excite me as much now as they did then, which has led to a desire to share them with others. My godmother, now retired but still very much part of my life, gave her consent on condition that I include with them some of the prayer-poems I wrote and sent to her at the time. Unbeknown to me, she had chosen to keep these poems safe over the years, just as I did her letters. When I told her I only now understand some of what she wrote to me then, she replied, typically, that she did not mind being a lady-in-waiting for the Holy Spirit!

So together we have made a selection of the letters and poems to tell the story of part of a journey – my journey into faith. Of course the rest of my life did not stand still meanwhile. I met my husband in Africa, soon after we graduated; and at present we live in Cornwall with our two growing children. My spiritual journey has continued, but never with the intensity of the student years – until now. I have a distinct feeling that rediscovering Ailsa's letters may just be about to change that!

Dear Kate,

It was so good to hear from you and to learn you have been provisionally accepted for university in the autumn. Your letter was a joy to receive but a real lesson in the inadequacy of words when trying to reply!

Asking me to 'tell you about prayer' is a bit like asking me to tell you about my life with David. Where does one begin? – except, perhaps, with that very analogy. For prayer is essentially a relationship, inspired by love and constantly growing and deepening, through which we learn to know someone who has always known everything about us! Have you ever heard the old song 'Getting to know you'…? Getting to know anybody means not doing all the talking but listening as well. Likewise with God! It's a pity the word 'prayer' has such narrowly religious connotations – something that good people do, in church or just before going to sleep. Prayer isn't just something we do in the intervals, Kate, but a whole new, exciting way of living, which makes every hour of the day holy. Writing an essay or doing the ironing becomes as much a prayer as if we were on our knees in church.

As you think about this, if you ask God directly, 'Lord, teach me to pray', then He will, and you will be setting out on the greatest adventure of your life. It may, or may not be, sweetness and roses, for prayer is no anaesthetic against life's natural buffeting. Rather it is through the things that happen to us that God teaches us, always with love. And the wonder of it is that the more you get to know Him, the more there is to find out! Dear Kate, you ask about prayer, yet your very questioning is the stirring of God's Spirit and a prayer in itself. He is always the initiator; at the most our prayer is only ever a response.

David and I celebrated our nineteenth wedding anniversary yesterday with a walk across the beach and a shared bottle of wine on a favourite cliff-top. The sunset was magnificent!

With much to be thankful for.

Your ever-loving godmother,

Ailsa

Dear Kate,

It was so good to hear from you again and so soon – in spite of your revision. It was good to hear my letter excited you. Yes, of course it's all right to get excited about God – I still do! Like falling in love, our relationship with Him is essentially that, a love story in which He may spend a good part of our life waiting patiently for us to just look at Him! But when we do, as you are doing now, Kate, then His look of love, even if we only perceive it dimly, can be both exciting and disturbing.

No, it's not written in stone that we must think of God as our Father, even though that was the image Jesus gave to his disciples. A lot depends on our personal experience of fatherhood and whether or not that works for us. God in Himself is neither father nor mother, nor brother, nor lover, but all our experiences of love together – and so much more! To each person He gives an image in which to think of Himself which best suits them, and indeed may change as we get to know Him. So, my dear Kate, if you get excited about God as Beloved (like the author of the Song of Songs), then that's fine and certainly does not exclude His qualities of fatherhood which you may also experience from time to time. Whatever the image we are given, it is only a means to greater intimacy with Himself. I think the excitement comes with realising our whole life is a short opportunity to say 'yes' to God's love. However ordinary that life may seem, every moment of it offers us an opportunity of meeting Him. This morning's post brought a card from a friend with a quotation from Elizabeth Barrett-Browning:

> *Earth's crammed with heaven,*
> *And every common bush afire with God;*
> *But only he who sees, takes off his shoes,*
> *The rest sit round it and pluck blackberries.*

I must stop here or I may canter off on a favourite hobby-horse of mine, that of discovering the extraordinary in the ordinary, sightings of which He will surely give you in the mystery of His friendship. For now, I assure you of my prayers, holding you daily in His light, with thanks for the beautiful person you are becoming.

My love as always,

Ailsa

Dear Kate,

Thank you for your most beautiful letter; the Holy Spirit is obviously very active in your life at present. As you rightly point out, love is always a risk, and pain often part of it. Last Christmas, a poster on our church door showed a new mother and her baby with the caption, 'Love anything at all and your heart will surely be wrung and possibly broken; if you want to keep it intact, you must give your heart to no-one, not even to an animal' (C.S. Lewis). One gentleman in our congregation said it was the biggest argument against Christianity he had ever seen!

Yes, love always seems to involve a willingness on our part to become vulnerable. Nearly always it requires that initial leap of faith where we have so much to take on trust. Whether we find it easy or not usually depends on our previous experiences. If we have been let down by people in the past, we may well find our ability to trust is impaired. I am reminded of helping with a session of psychodrama where the participants were invited to place themselves where they thought they were on an imaginary line of trust, going from 0% – 100% across the room. In this group of people with mental health problems, every single person placed themselves towards the bottom end of the scale. Significant, isn't it? Trust is a beautiful but fragile thing, involving contact (albeit unconsciously) with our inner child, and if that child has been hurt, then healing will be needed alongside any growth in intimacy. It's interesting that Jesus encourages us to become like little children, whose capacity for trust is their most obvious characteristic. However, we should be careful to remember (as many have said) that He didn't encourage us to stay like children – because that would only be an excuse to avoid the pain of growing up.

To 'become' a little child is very different and demands courage. It involves a trust and simplicity which lie the other side of complicatedness and, if we are honest, are not easily won. It means a coming to acceptance of things as they really are – especially ourselves, 'warts and all'! Then we arrive at a childlike lightness and wonder, with a sense that everything is ultimately in good hands. To meet a person for whom this has become a reality is always a delight.

So any growth in intimacy, whether with friend, lover or God, involves a journey in trust. Dear

Kate, it's wonderful that you are able to take this leap of faith and see it as an adventure. Of course, Abraham is our role model here; he went out into the unknown at the call of God, trusting only God and His promise. Bon voyage, my dear! Listen to the voice that speaks low, just below the level of hearing, and calls you 'beloved' in the depths of your heart – and trust it.

All my love, and always prayer,

Ailsa

Dearest Kate,

Thank you for your card from the middle of a very busy week, where you express your concern that God could be edged out in the flurry of demands made upon you. You say you hesitate to set aside specific time for prayer because you want your relationship with God to be spontaneous, as that's the sort of person you are and it's how you relate to others.

Yes, and I do thank God for that spontaneity which allows His Spirit to move in you. However, we are talking here about building a relationship, and if we are serious about getting to know anyone, then we need to make time for them. And just as times spent alone together cement and nourish friendship, so it is with God. Although every second of daily life is infused with His presence, we can only relate to Him in that hurly-burly when we also spend time alone with Him. Remember *The Little Prince*, the book by Antoine de Saint-Exupéry? (I know you are familiar with it.) The little Prince learned that the task of winning the trust and friendship of the fox could be accomplished only by coming to meet him at the same time each day.

So, my dear Kate, may I suggest you make a date with God, arrange a time and place where you will be, just for Him. Of course, this doesn't need to be a church – even better if it isn't! – just a secret place, indoors or out, known only to the two of you. Finding a place is prayer in itself, an expression of your love and desire for Him. All He then asks is your willingness to be there, and He will be waiting for you. Whatever happens next will be up to Him. Listen, and trust your heart. You need no words, only to be open to Him, and willing. An old French priest, the Curé d'Ars, used to spend long hours in front of the altar, and when asked what he did there all the time replied, 'I look at Him and He looks at me, and we tell one another we love each other'. One of the most profound descriptions ever, I think.

Thinking of you amidst all the sixth form business and demands on your time. Working from a busy social workers' office, I am well tuned into you!

Lots of love – and with you in prayer,

Ailsa

Dear Kate,

So, the exams are over and all we have to do is wait for the results to see where the future will take you.

It's strange you yourself should be in a waiting phase when you ask about the validity of 'waiting' in prayer. As you are experiencing, waiting is very much part of everyday living, and we don't like it! But as with everything else in our lives, God can use it to draw us closer to Himself. We don't like waiting because somehow it disempowers us, yet it can be a very creative thing. Carlo Carretto, someone worth reading, who gave up his professional life to live with God in the desert, says, 'For me to pray means to wait.' What did he mean? Well, creative waiting is about being receptive. It is actually a basic condition of our meeting God. Doesn't your friend T.S. Eliot say, 'The faith and the love and the hope are all in the waiting'? As part of our training in the school of God's love, waiting helps us learn to hand over control to Him, by accepting that He comes (and goes!) in His own good time, as He thinks best. Sometimes we might spend most of our prayer time waiting for Him, in the same way a naturalist might wait for the coming of a rare and beautiful bird.

But do I sense in you a wanting to get on with things, Kate? It's very natural, and reminds me of Craig when he was young, helping David plant the beans. When they reached the end of the row, he straightaway went back to the beginning and dug them up again to see if they had grown! There is always the temptation to run ahead of God or to fill the spaces that waiting gives us. But when we wait in prayer, we wait in love for the Beloved, knowing He has waited for all time for this moment of our being there.

And sometimes He asks us to wait with Him as He asked his friends in the garden of Gethsemane, and we then find ourselves alongside our Lord, facing the world and its pain. This is a vocation in itself, but maybe more of that at a later time. For now, I hope this may help you to see that this kind of waiting is not only valid but is actually a vital part of prayer.

Will wait to hear news of your results.

Meanwhile, with you in the waiting.

With my love – as always,

Ailsa

My very dear Kate,

Thank you for your letter; I am so glad you wrote. Because I love you so much, I would like to give you a big hug and take away the pain of these first weeks away from home in a big city and university. However, something tells me that would not ultimately be in your best interests. So this is a hug of reassurance in an envelope!

I cannot help but feel your pain. Homesickness is one of the most desolate of experiences, emphasising that lonely place deep within each of us where we feel that we don't really matter. Nothing can prepare us for the initial shock of being in this place, and yet it is very natural that these first weeks away from a loving family and community should take you there. If nothing else, I want to reassure you that the pain you feel is directly connected with your growth as a person. You say your only comfort comes when you are sitting in stillness before God, and I take heart in this, confident that this sad time will pass for you and that God will use it as opportunity for you to grow in intimacy with Himself. For He does come to us in and through

24

the things that happen to us, and whatever life gives us, gives us God.

We long for intimacy, to be heard, to be known in the very depths of ourselves. And to some extent we are always lonely in this life because only the fullest union with God can meet our need. However, a growing relationship with Him does relieve our condition, and time spent in His company eventually changes loneliness to contentment. So hang in there, dear Kate, and I am sure the present pain will ease as you get to know more people and familiarise yourself with your new environment. The great thing is that you are not running away, either literally or through constant busyness. And when you do turn your face to God you are in a privileged position: you can also bring with you all the other young people who are homesick and lonely at this time.

Do keep in touch. I am constantly thinking of you, and as a favourite hymn says:

At the turn of each tide
He is there at my side
And His touch is as gentle as silence.

With all my love, and daily prayer,

Ailsa

Dear Kate,

I was so glad to receive your letter and to hear you are feeling so much better. You have done well to stick it out for a term before going home, and I am sure this Christmas will be a memorable homecoming for you. How lovely that your sister and family will be there too. It makes the season extra special to have small children in the house.

I do share your feelings about the consumerism of Christmas, but our pain can be nothing compared to God's pain at being ignored or unrecognised by the people He loves so much. Perhaps when we acknowledge our pain (as you have done) it then becomes possible to unite it to His, to join Him in His vulnerability as He abandons Himself into human hands. It is the most amazing thing that God came to us as a baby, so ordinary and unprotected, leaving power and glory behind so we wouldn't be afraid of Him. Wow! That's love! And it is as if each year at this time we are invited to see a little further into that mystery of His coming.

I do love Advent especially. Such a hidden time of stillness and quiet, a pulse of light waiting in darkness to be born, and, as yet, most of the world unaware of its coming. Hiddenness seems to be a vital ingredient of intimacy, and always the way God chooses for His coming – a stable, a carpenter's home, an upper room. People around had no idea what was taking place in their midst, what extraordinary events were happening beneath the shadow of ordinary daily life. But now, as then, some people are given eyes to see. For them, and for you, Kate, the baby in a stable seeks and meets them in the miracle of the everyday, where in ever-deepening intimacy, hidden from the world's eyes, He reveals to them who He is.

Goodness, I do go on! But I am confident you will discover the Christ-child beneath the tinselled trappings of Christmas and will welcome Him in the stable of your heart. We will meet in spirit around the altar on Christmas Eve and I shall be thinking of you throughout the holiday. Have a wonderful time! I look forward to you sharing some of your poems.

Love and prayer always,

Ailsa

DAISIES

I watch him stumbling up the path,

his tousled head bent,

his precious purpose cupped in his hands.

In readiness I kneel at the door.

Glowing face and grubby fingers thrust

the crudely plucked posy to my outstretched arms.

Loose-leafed images of his love,

the dismembered petals charm my soul

and fill my waiting heart with joy.

Is it thus, Lord, you kneel,

to receive our crumpled offering?

TWO-PINT BUCKET

I watch him and smile,
this tiny sun-clad figure
toddling purposefully down the beach,
on his way
to gather the whole ocean
in his two-pint plastic bucket.

Do you smile too, Lord,
at the pursuits
of our infancy,
when we try to contain you
in things we understand
and can hold in our hand?

A JOURNEY

It was a bad day for a journey;
the heavens hung howling round the
                              rain-racked roadway
as we sped our way westward
through the sodden, storm-clad countryside.
Yet, absorbed in his games,
he played unconcerned,
our small boy,
secure and content in the car.

Knowing neither the why nor the way of
                              our journey,
there were no anxious questions such as
'Where are we going?' or 'Where are we now?'
His father was driving and nothing else mattered!
With trust born of childhood
came certainty of safety,
that with him in control
all, indeed, would be well.

Dear Kate,

Many thanks for your post-Christmas letter and poems. I was so impressed by your thoughts on sharing Christmas with the children and what you felt they had taught you about your relationship with God. You have obviously identified yourself with the invitation from Christ to 'become like a little child', and I loved the qualities you recognised in your young nephews which apply to your own spiritual life. Your poem about the car journey with him in the back was so evocative; no anxiety about where he was going or what the weather would be like, he had the 'trust born of childhood' so that 'his father was driving and nothing else mattered'. Wonderful! And your comment that small children only live in the present was completely on the ball. 'Whether happy or not, only the present moment was real for him, he lived completely in the "now".' The sacrament of the present moment indeed! If only we didn't lose it as we grow up – and have to start learning it all over again!

How marvellous that you are having a 'listening break' with a few friends before returning to university. Your friend's family cottage sounds delightful, and listening to the dawn chorus a beautiful way to begin the day, especially followed by breakfast together. I think the first meal of the day is so important, especially when shared. David and I often have a silent breakfast and find it offers a good basis for the day, especially if it's to be a particularly hectic one. And I love the thought of Jesus cooking breakfast for his friends on the beach. Your evenings spent sharing around the log fire, which you so beautifully evoke, are a form of prayer in themselves, because where two or three meet together 'at the ground of their being' there is God also.

I can see you are discovering 'listening' as an essential ingredient in all deepening relationships and that certainly includes our relationship with God. St Benedict, the founder of Western monasticism, begins the Rule of Life he wrote for his monks with that very word, 'Listen'. It is a sign of good relationship, isn't it, if you can be together without carrying on a non-stop conversation? And it can be very moving to witness an elderly couple who have been together very many years, sitting with each other in silent contentment. Yet this situation with a partner is hard-won, as it is in our relationship with God, and learning to listen to either is the work of a lifetime.

To listen deeply, we need not only silence, but stillness, firstly in our immediate surroundings and ultimately within our hearts. The latter is not easily arrived at and is ultimately God's gift to us. And, of course, initially when we settle down to listen to Him, we can find our souls anything but quiet –

They pitch in from every side
a razzmatazz of voices
clamouring for attention;
the Church says ... and the family says ...
the committee'd community and society says ...
and from deep within our darkest interior
jungle voices of nature
rise up to join in
My Lord, did you speak?
My God, I can't hear you!
Has your silence been strangled
and slaughtered by sound?

Enjoy Cornwall, Kate, and the still moments of friendship.

Thinking of you there.

With love – as always,

Ailsa

Dear Kate,

You ask me to tell you more about silence and how it is possible to become still within. My immediate response would be 'with great difficulty'! But later you mention that you and your friend have decided to 'go on retreat' to the community of Tymawr.* How wonderful! This actual experience of silence will teach you so much more than anything I could tell you. We could *talk* about it forever. It's like being thirsty; in the end only taking a drink will relieve it. I am so pleased you have decided to go to Tymawr, because apart from knowing and loving the place and its people, I know you will benefit from the support of a stable community. The monastic offices will provide a framework for your time, where you will find yourselves joining in prayer that is already going on, and should you wish to speak privately to any of the Sisters, that is easily arranged. I am glad too that you have decided to be silent for most of the time but just

---

* A contemplative community of nuns living in Wales.

meet together for meals – that sounds a very balanced way to begin. And of course God Himself will be there to meet you, for silence is the language of prayer. I always used to say to Him before my visits there, 'I'm not going looking for you, but will be there if you want me.' He never disappoints.

However, to answer your question a little more directly. There are techniques that can be used to help us become still, but nothing comparable to what you will be doing at Tymawr – jumping in at the deep end! We've talked before about the need to set aside specific times to be silent before God, and hopefully these times will eventually spill over and affect the whole of our lives. We're talking about the work of a lifetime. Some people find it helpful to use a mantra to quieten the mind. An example of this is the Jesus prayer, 'Lord Jesus Christ, Son of God, have mercy on me a sinner', used as a whole or in part, repeating it over and over silently. You may prefer to use a single word, 'Lord' or 'Jesus' or 'Maranatha' (Greek for 'Come, Lord') to pierce the Cloud of Unknowing* between ourselves and God.

---

* *The Cloud of Unknowing*, a fourteenth-century classic in the tradition of silent contemplative prayer.

I should emphasise that the mantra, and even the silence to which it may lead, is itself no more than a tool to help us in our journey to God, and doesn't suit everyone. The greatest aid is our desire to pray, our setting aside the clatter of life with the intention of listening for that still small voice. In many ways, if you want to pray, then you are already doing so. And of course, the real answer to your question is, 'Keep at it!'

I think of you so often.

With love and thanksgiving,

Ailsa

A SMALL WOODEN BALL

A small wooden ball
at the tips of my fingers,
twirling the world
in the palm of a hand:
perfect precision
sandalwood symmetry
each grain a granule
of the glory of the world.

And today fits in
somewhere
to this wonder of oneness
the sigh of a sparrow
falling frozen to the ground
a splinter
of the splendour
of the glory of the whole.

Dear Kate,

Many thanks for your letter received this week enclosing your lovely poem about the wooden ball, so reminiscent of Julian of Norwich. As for what you say about the criticism you've been getting, in a way I have been half expecting something like this to crop up, ever since you told me that you were going to Tymawr. When someone becomes serious about prayer to the extent of going on retreat, then inevitably, sooner or later, someone will accuse them of navel-gazing, or selfishly ignoring the needs of the world to satisfy their personal pursuit of peace. Such accusations almost always come from people who have not yet experienced the paradox that prayer equips us better to face up to the needs of our world, whether distant or near at hand.

Yet such accusations do make us stop and think. For many years I was unable to say the Jesus prayer without substituting 'us' for 'me'. That was until a wise person suggested that when we say 'have mercy on me', we really mean ourselves as part of the whole, whether it be family, community or simply humankind. And that makes sense, because there is no such thing as a private prayer and even when we are physically alone we pray as part of a larger world beyond ourselves. It is significant that when the disciples asked Jesus to teach them to pray, He told them to say 'Our Father'. It is my belief that when we turn our face to God from wherever we may be, whatever the situation or mood in which we find ourselves, then somehow we bring to Him not only ourselves but many others: people who are in the same place as we are but maybe looking the other way. As a river carries all it meets to the depths of the sea, so we carry with us all our concerns and companions into the ocean of God's love. This is possibly the most important thing we can do for another person. And we are never alone in this vocation of prayer, but united on the prayer-waves with all others doing the same. Ultimately, of course, we all join in the prayer of Jesus, which He is continuously making to the Father on our behalf. And it is together with Him that we weave a welcome, offer a space for God to enter the life of the world.

Now you have really got me going! I see more and more, though, that through prayer God offers us a way of sharing in His work in the world. Far from being meaningful only to ourselves, a growing relationship with our Lord has deep significance for the life of our friends and for the world at large. Mystery indeed!

Give my love to Sister Veronica Ann at Tymawr.

I shall be thinking of you there.

With all my love and ongoing prayer,

Ailsa

You are the underground spring

that flows through the moments of my day,

unseen beneath the surface of each least encounter,

giving glory to little things

through the current of your love.

But here in the stillness of this solitary place

you burst from beneath

to rise shimmering in sunlight –

torrent of tenderness fresh-flowering the desert,

silent stream of love flooding the earth.

My dear Kate,

Many thanks for the postcard and poem from Tymawr, and for your letter a few days after you came back.

I am so glad you found God waiting for you there and that you fell in love both with Him and with the place. I somehow thought you might! Apart from the physical beauty of the landscape, there's something so supportive about being with a loving, praying community, and I understand well your experience of 'underneath are the everlasting arms', made tangible through that community. I empathise only too well with your reluctance to leave, your tears and fear of loss. In the story of Jesus' transfiguration, when it was time to go down from the mountain, Peter, James and John wanted to stay at the top and build memorials there to their experience. So we're in good company!

It is indeed wonderful, dear Kate, that God has touched you at such depths, yet, loving you as I do, I am also very sensitive to your post-retreat pain. The reality is that God is with you today in the hurly-burly of a university campus just as much as at Tymawr, only covered up by more layers of living. You say you don't want to lose the closeness you experienced there, and that is very natural. But it is this very desire for intimacy with Himself that God will use to draw you further along that path. It may seem to us that He comes and goes, but in fact he doesn't go away at all. Perhaps He allows us to feel like that so our desire for Him will grow, until the time that our hearts are large and empty enough to receive all the love we need. It isn't an easy path (as you're beginning to discover) and pain accompanies the longing, but that very longing is a sign of growth more than all our pleasant feelings. It is indeed the journey of your life, and one helped by friendship with communities like Tymawr. Someone once said to me, 'We grow like those we spend time with.' My reply was 'Here's hoping!' It's of great help to remember that the life of prayer, work and study will continue there every day until your next visit, and you can tune in at any time – I know the Sisters will be tuning in and praying for you, Kate.

How amazing that Merlin, the convent cat, came and sat in your chair – the ultimate sign of acceptance! Yes, the library is great, and it seems significant that the book which 'fell off the shelf' for you was Brother Lawrence's: *The Practice of the Presence of God.* In many ways we need no more for our journey. This seventeenth-century French monk mastered the practice so well that his times in the kitchen were no different from times in chapel; his whole life became a prayer. Someone like that is worth listening to!

Don't worry too much about letting go of God, because He will never let go of you.

You are always in my love and prayer,

Ailsa

Dear Kate,

It was good to hear from you – as always! – but I was sorry to hear about your friend who is ill in hospital in London and do hope it can be arranged for you to visit her. Wasn't she one of the people who joined you in your listening break at the end of your first semester?

It's perfectly natural for you to be asking questions about intercessory prayer at a time like this. I'll do my best to throw you a few pointers, but basically it's a mystery to me too! As I see it, intercession is simply standing in the presence of God for the sake of another, and then leaving the outcome in His hands. In essence all prayer is intercession because of our interconnectedness, which we've spoken of before. And sometimes, because there seems to be so much trouble in the world, it appears more fruitful to concentrate on our relationship with God and leave it to Him to use our offering in whichever way He sees best.

Having said that, individual needs and concerns of those close to our hearts are important too, and I believe God allows us to join His Son in compassionate entreaty for them. A particularly good parable of this is the story of the paralysed man in the gospels, whose friends, unable to get through the crowds, lowered him through the roof to Jesus' feet. They then left him there. Our problem is that we don't really believe it works! We cannot believe God would take any notice of our pleas, certainly not to the extent of them affecting the outcome of events. Our faith is really very small, but I am convinced that it has something to do with God allowing us to share in His loving concern for people and thus becoming part of a movement towards their ultimate good. The problem lies in the fact that we do not see things the way God does, and what we think would be someone's ultimate good is often very different from God's plan for them. Our imagination cannot stretch to what God has in mind and all we are left with is trust. From within that, I believe there is nothing more important we can do for an individual or for our world than to hold their life before God.

Some people are called to make this their life's work and in some mysterious way become an intercession themselves. This thought struck me as I watched a Tymawr Sister spreading manure on the rose-bed. What she was doing was quite simple – she would go into the field, fill the barrow, wheel it back and empty the contents on the border before digging it in. This she did time and time again, but she did it all with the whole of herself, soul and body, and she did it for God. She embodied for me then the Shantidera (the favourite prayer of a thirteenth-century Dalai Lama):

For as long as space endures
And for as long as living beings remain,
Until then may I too abide
To dispel the misery of the world.

I do hope this isn't more than you can digest, Kate, but I know you enjoy something to chew on! Just as an afterthought, I am reminded of a statue of God in Chartres Cathedral which I often mention if someone asks, 'Where is God in all this suffering?' It's a beautiful sculpture of God on the seventh day of creation, and He has one silent tear rolling down the contours of His face.

Holding your friend Maggie in prayer and thanking God for your loving concern.

All my love,

Ailsa

PADDINGTON

'Where does your business go
when it leaves London?
Nowhere? Nowhere fast?'
The train arriving at platform four
is the four-twenty to
nowhere?

People commuting, souls in transit,
all going somewhere
and anxious to get there;
tickets purchased,
routes decided,
destination assured.

But the ticket you've given me is blank!
Alone in the hubbub,
lost amidst the directed confusion,
panic chases fear to be first to greet me.
Must I travel without knowing the route?
Board a train that may take me nowhere?

Cast helpless in iron, Brunel sits watching,
quietly ignored by his bustling creation;
while the Maker of men, though also passed by,
moves active and free in the world that He made.
'Trust me! I purchased your ticket with my life;
you have no need of any itinerary,
for I shall be travelling with you
and will show you the way you are to go!'

JUST LOVE

Watching and waiting,
alone with the sparrows
beneath the towering branches of this great London
                                                    hospital,
they come and they go,
white-coated, starch-capped, purposeful people,
en route to important work in service of the
                                                    community.

No one looks twice
at the grey-scarfed old lady shuffling past my seat,
but she stops
and she smiles
and she speaks to this stranger.
Her smile is Christ's smile
and her gentleness His touch;
does she know what she's giving in passing?
No badge of profession;
too old for a job.
Her vocation? Just love.

Dear Kate,

Many thanks for your letter giving me news of Maggie and your visit to her. Thank you too for the poems you included. I especially loved the one about Paddington Station – so expressive, and finding echoes in my own heart. Do keep writing and please keep sharing them.

Your question, 'Is it possible to live like Brother Lawrence and the Sisters at Tymawr while living in the world?' puts you slap bang in the centre of the spiritual quest of the twenty-first-century. Communities generally are becoming smaller, while people like ourselves seem drawn to them in droves, not for the most part with the intention of joining them, but of finding there some light on the question you have asked. And it does seem that this is the way the Spirit is leading. I would feel very inadequate even to attempt an answer if I did not believe God Himself was in this exchange between us. Mother Teresa of Calcutta used to say: 'He can write beautifully with even the most broken of pens.' So here goes!

I think the question you are asking is whether those of us outside convent walls can aspire to that depth and closeness of relationship with God that you have witnessed (and even experienced yourself) there. To begin with, it's important to realise that monks and nuns don't live on a permanent spiritual 'high', but rather their darkness can be even deeper than ours because they have no distractions. Having said that, they do seem to have it all set up, don't they? – life organised in such a way that God is the centre and raison d'être of everything and they, without our commitments, are thus enabled to be full-time seekers.

It was our friend St Benedict who started the whole thing off in the sixth century by founding what he called 'a school of the Lord's service' and writing a Rule of Life for his monks, its pupils. Everything then, as now, was ordered to foster the qualities deemed necessary for development of the spiritual life through poverty, humility, simplicity, hiddenness (does any of this sound familiar?). And everything was to be done with moderation and in love, this being the end to which it was all directed. It's this same Benedict who can help in answering your question, because he's as relevant to our life in the world today as to sixth-century asceticism. This is because – and I find this so exciting! – the school of the Lord's service doesn't exist simply in convents and monasteries. It is the School of Life and the business of everyday living, through which God provides all we need for our journey to Himself. Whether we live inside or outside convent walls, is a matter of choice or calling rather than degrees of holiness. The Holy Spirit leads us all, if we are willing, over exactly the same spiritual terrain and Benedict's wisdom is able to shed light on our paths as much as it did for his monks. And it's for everyone, whether they recognise the fact or not! But for those given eyes to see, already following Benedict's exhortation 'Listen', and who are passionate about their relationship with God, the wonder of their gradually growing closer to God may be consciously entered into. For them, everything becomes an occasion of grace and all things work together for good. It is then that our heart becomes our cell and monasticism is interiorised. As we prepare ourselves to receive Him through silence and prayer, God uses the things that happen in our daily life, just as He uses their particular form of life for the monastics, to lead us all to Himself.

I want so much to communicate all this to you, Kate, but am finding it difficult without turning this letter into an essay! Take poverty for example. Consciously chosen by monastics as an aid towards freedom of spirit, it comes to us of its own accord, though in many disguises. Life provides its own poverty, which can mean so many things as well as physical hunger and homelessness. It can mean lack of space or silence, tiredness or loneliness, the feeling of being outside life, or of being just a number. Basically, poor people are anonymous and unimportant – a felt experience life offers most of us at some time or another. Then there's simplicity, the getting rid of non-essentials which Benedict implies we learn to do in all aspects of our life. Sickness of any sort does the job naturally for us; and many ordinary people feel that if they could sit in the middle of a field without any possessions but free from pain or anxiety, that would be enough for them.

Oh dear! I'm afraid this may have become like an essay inspite of myself. And I could go on! But I'll restrain myself and point you instead to Esther de Waal's *Seeking God: The Way of St Benedict*. Far more eloquent than I could ever be, she will take you from here. But thank you for your question, the answer to which is Yes! The essence of the spiritual life lived so beautifully by Brother Lawrence and the Tymawr Sisters can be yours. Everything and all life is holy, as I believe you know already, dearest Kate. I do hope this isn't all too much gobbledy-gook.

The first poppy bloomed in our garden today, I always feel it's a sign from the Holy Spirit.

Love and prayer,

Ailsa

THIS DAISY

Just to be
like this daisy
common flower of the field
that's content just to be
and receive
what it is.
Without striving or argument
it raises its head
in the great congregation
who worship their Maker
by being
what they are.

Of little account, they never win prizes,
these little flowers of God's own creation;
not treasured, though precious,
their beauty's disregarded
and their glory trodden underfoot.
Yet
tuned in by nature
to the choir of creation
they celebrate your purpose
by being
what they are.

Dear Kate,

Thank you so much for your letter and beautiful 'Daisy' poem. They taught me a lot, especially when you thanked me for my beautiful words but said you didn't think they could ever apply to you. I was stopped in my tracks! It made me realise that in my excitement at your openness and natural understanding of the spiritual journey, I had overrun myself (and you). Instead of listening to your heartbeat, I had danced off on my own track, and can now only trust the Holy Spirit to put my mistake right.

When you said you wonder whether you're up to all this there was an echo in my head of my early stays at Tymawr when, feeling much the same as you, I went for a walk in the woods. I thought, I will never be up to this in the way the Sisters and some other guests are; I feel so inadequate! Then, amongst the great tall-reaching trees, I came across a clearing where a small and very young sapling was just coming into leaf. I felt God telling me it was all right to be little and vulnerable, because I belonged, and was of value to Him and to the rest of the wood. Only much later came acceptance of littleness and subsequent rejoicing in it.

So, in some way, I welcome what you say because the beginning of self-acceptance (basic to real spiritual growth) is often an experience of our own littleness, brokenness or 'not being up to this'. It is really only then that God can get to work on us, so to speak. It seems the way He chooses to do that is always through some need we have. A well-known illustration of this is of the apparently perfect novice breaking down in floods of tears and the Reverend Mother sighing with relief, 'There's hope for you yet!' In this light, as entrances for God's approach, our vulnerability and weakness, far from being something of which to be ashamed, become to us a cause for thanksgiving.

One more monastic reflection to finish! When asked what they do all day in the monastery, one very wise abbot replied, 'We fall down and get up, and fall down and get up!'

Thinking of you so much.

With love and prayer,

Ailsa

Dear Kate,

Well, yes, indeed. Why does it always seem to be about need and weakness, and even dying? And is the church just made up of needy people? What about success and beauty and creativity? My goodness, you do keep my little grey cells working! And once again I shall have to call on the Holy Spirit to interpret what I can only express very inarticulately.

As I'm sure I've said before, I think the bottom line for all of us is acceptance of ourselves as we are, warts and all. All of us, whether or not we are aware, are wounded in one way or another by ordinary events of living. And our growth in the spiritual journey usually coincides with a growing awareness of such wounds which tends to surface in the silence of prayer. When this happens, healing has begun and although it may feel painful it is a reason for rejoicing.

It would seem this is how God has made us. Wanting us to come to Him freely, He creates vulnerable individuals, but uses our very neediness to woo us and draw us to Himself. This is perhaps the place to mention false humility, in itself a characteristic of so many people with low self-esteem and a compulsion to put themselves down. Nelson Mandela has expressed this beautifully (though I'm only quoting from memory): 'Our deepest fear is not that we are inadequate. Our deepest fear is that we are powerful beyond belief. It is our light, not our darkness that most frightens us. You are a child of God and your playing small doesn't serve the world. We are all meant to shine as children do. We are born to manifest the glory of God within us. It is not just in some of us, it is in everyone. And as we let our light shine, we unconsciously give other people permission to do the same.'

Not always what we get from the pulpit on a Sunday morning, I agree! Indeed, the Church often seems to emphasise sin rather than joy, and it's by the latter we should be recognised. It is one of God's greatest gifts, yet we often forget He wants us to be happy. On occasions we may have to make a conscious decision to receive it – for joy is always a gift, and more often than not a big surprise.

My very dear Kate, what will the Holy Spirit do with all this, I wonder? Whatever else He does I hope He will communicate the great love and hope with which it is written.

We must be keeping the post office in business!

My love always. And please pray for me,

Ailsa

Dear Kate,

Many thanks for your beautiful card and letter carrying assurances that the Holy Spirit has already made up for my failings. You have such a generous heart and I'm so glad you are beginning to recognise vulnerability and weakness as possible positives and channels for God's grace. (And glad you approve so heartily of Mandela!)

I love the fact that you have a photo on your desk of your young nephew, arms open wide, running across the beach, and your comment 'maybe he can teach me how to live'. The Holy Spirit is not far from you, Kate, and it's so good you are recognising His presence in daily life with your heart as well as your mind. Someone once said that the fact God chose to live as a carpenter in Nazareth is more amazing than the Resurrection. I expect I've mentioned Sister Paula's dictum which I use as an unwritten, silent agenda during my work in community mental health. It is simply, 'Every least en-counter is a gesture of His; a means of giving and receiving Christ Himself.' When I first met her, Sister Paula was guest mistress at Tymawr and able to hold her own with the cleverest of minds, but a series of strokes disabled her and she ended her life in the convent infirmary, helpless as a baby but still gracious. Contrary to appearances, those who loved this wonderful lady realised that now she was at the pinnacle of her vocation, exemplifying God's power made perfect in weakness.

Maybe I have over reached myself yet again, but now I can trust the Holy Spirit to make it right, just as I can trust Him to lead you on your journey. Dearest Kate, you are a great inspiration to me.

With all my love and thanksgiving,

Ailsa

Dear Kate,

A beautiful surprise arrived in the post this morning! Of course you may bring your new friend, Adam, to stay. We are delighted and look forward to seeing you both.

How wonderful that Adam's Scottish heritage has opened up the world of Celtic spirituality for you. Yes indeed, Pembrokeshire is a great place to research and to experience it. I've always been aware of the imaginary line connecting Iona and St David's because the same spirit permeates both. Standing on a cliff-top in either place, it's easy to understand the heart of the Celtic tradition beating in time with the turning tides and gale force winds. I well understand and share your attraction, Kate. Celtic spirituality embodies so much of where you are now, and can only enrich your journey. Here all life is holy (and each day a feast day!) interconnected and encircled by the Divine. Echoes of Brother Lawrence? The liturgy, as you will find, includes prayers for ordinary, everyday events such as dressing, lighting a fire, welcoming friends or setting off on a journey.

But you yourselves will discover all this and so much more. We have jewels in this far west peninsula: many scattered ancient Celtic churches, the embodiment of simplicity and fitting in so well with the landscape. Often hidden away, they never distract us from nature herself. A few years ago a local priest used to take a group of us on pilgrimage around these little churches, ending with a Eucharist on the headland before retiring to a local hostelry in good, Celtic tradition! We will enjoy showing them to you; it's such a privilege to live amidst this vibrant landscape.

Until then, take care, and in the words of a Celtic blessing for those setting out on a journey,

> *May the road rise to meet you*
> *the wind be always at your back,*
> *may the sun shine warm upon your face*
> *the rain fall soft upon your fields*
> *and until we meet again*
> *may God keep you in the palm of His hand.*

Very much love and thoughts of you,

Ailsa

Dearest Kate and Adam,

Our cottage is strangely silent today and we miss you. It was so good to have you with us and to share your delight both in each other and the surrounding landscape. The Celtic tradition really came to life for you, didn't it? It was great exploring with you the little churches on the ancient 'saints and stones' trail, and your pilgrimage to St David's along the old pilgrim and coastal route will be especially memorable, I'm sure. You are right, the Celtic heartbeat is almost tangible in certain places in this peninsula. That was a special moment in the little church at Haroldson West, wasn't it? – an especially 'thin' place, where the spirit of St Aidan is surely still around.

As you say, next time we must visit Caldey, island of saints, since you've heard so much about it! It warmed my heart to hear of your interest in the Cistercian tradition, but we had better leave that for another time or your spirit could be going into overload! But yes, it is one of the hidden treasures of our Church and has lots to say to us lay-people.

My dears, thank you again for your visit. It was so good to have you with us and to be caught up in your energy and enthusiasm.

Look after each other

and much love to you both,

Ailsa

CADER IDRIS

We hadn't chosen the path,
the path chose us
to follow its treacherous track
to the top of the Idris.

We hadn't meant to come this way;
ill-equipped for climbing and bad weather,
we'd set off in sunshine
to meander gently the innocent slopes
of this giant Welshman.
But somewhere, sometime, we'd strayed from
                                    that path
and the way to the summit lay before us.
Realising its direction,
yet still within reach of the lake-lapped slopes,
we'd answered 'yes' to the call of the mountain.

It seems we've been climbing forever

when we notice night

stalking our path and preparing for plunder;

trapped in our tracks and prisoned in panic,

we hide our face in the rock

and hang hope from the heart-beat of the mountain.

Dawn does come

with the clearness of newness,

and the wonder of silence ranged round the jewel

of Tal-y-Llyn

is one more miracle along the way.

Love grows

from the hard rock of this treacherous track,

and we give thanks in the way

for the joy of the way.

NURTURE

Still you are there
on a day weaved with wanting and wishing things
                                    different,
where nothing is right and we can't seem to win;
still you are there
silent in the shadows of the present situation,
when we're faced with our failure
and fear of love.
And you kneel as mother
to receive our heart's offering,
accepting with love
the young child we are still;
and you nurture this child
through each step of her growing,
loving her littleness
and the person she will become.

Dear Kate,

Thank you so much for your last little batch of poems. You really do seem to have hit on a medium for expressing your innermost thoughts and feelings. Thank you for sharing them. I love them all because they are part of you, but I think 'Cader Idris' is my favourite yet. Apart from the fact that I love the place, it reminds me of Eliot's *Journey of the Magi* – 'A cold coming we had of it ...' Keep writing – I am savouring and saving every one!

Thank you too for the beautiful poppy card. When you wrote of a feeling of deep connectedness between us I was reminded of friendship in the Celtic tradition and their evocative word, *anam cara* (*anam* is Gaelic for soul, and *cara* their word for friend). With your *anam cara* you could share your innermost self, relate as you really were and be unconditionally understood and accepted. It is always God's gift and ultimately He is the *anam cara* of each of us, but allows us another to support us on our journey to Him. Such friendship crosses age gaps as well as oceans and I thank Him for your love, Kate, as my spirit dances alongside yours.

Give Adam my love. I wonder how things are going and hope you are still enjoying life together.

With my love as always

and thanksgiving for our friendship,

Ailsa

Dear Kate,

Please forgive my not replying immediately to your letter, but the question you raise is so important that I wanted to gather my thoughts and pray over them first.

You speak about a tension you feel between your spiritual life and your relationship with Adam. This is so important and so relevant at a time when the Holy Spirit is calling lay-people, as well as the 'professionally' religious ones, to a life of prayer and union with God. I identify with so much of what you say, having lived in the same house as God and David for twenty years! Your letter touched me deeply because, as usual, you express so vividly the yearnings of those not drawn to a celibate or religious life, but still called to this deeply intimate relationship with God.

The thing is, Kate, that your relationship with Adam is very much part of your spiritual life. Somebody once said that there are not two loves, the one for relating to God and the other for relationships with people. All life, and certainly all loving is equally holy and God is as present in your relationship with Adam as when you're on your knees in prayer. For where love is, there God is – as you know really. An old hero of mine (one time vicar of our parish) got up to speak at his Golden Wedding, and began: 'There have always been three of us in this marriage!' Yet I do understand the tension you speak of when you say Adam is more of an 'active' Christian and doesn't understand your leaning to the contemplative way. I believe it's important in any relationship to be conscious of our differences – but then to delight in them. Your contemplative life and Adam's more active way could turn out to be a wonderful combination, if you nurture as well as respect your differences. You could become a great team. The most important thing is that we are allowed the freedom to be ourselves; I don't think you or I could manage without that! – but that also involves allowing our partners the same freedom. So often I have come across women who have tried to drag their partners along with them on their spiritual quest, and it's been disastrous for both of them. Did you know that in Hebrew one of the words for salvation is also the word for space? Appropriate, don't you think? And Kahlil Gibran says,

Let there be spaces in your togetherness,
for the winds of heaven to dance between you.

So in answer to your query as to how I have managed a spiritual life as well as a husband, the answer is: mainly due to the qualities of my husband who has allowed my spirit the freedom to be – as well as embodying the kind of virtues we're always talking about.

Tensions, if that's all it is, can be creative, Kate. Another hero of mine, Harry Williams, a Mirfield monk who was responsible for the prayers at Prince Charles' and Diana's wedding, has written a book called *Tensions* in which he claims they are not only a necessary part of living but essential for our growth as human beings. The holiest response, which he saves for the last chapter, is laughter! Not a laughing at or a social type of giggling, but the result of not taking ourselves too seriously, and living with the lightness of people very close to our Lord.

My dear Kate, I don't apologise this time for the length of this letter. The subject is important; holy ground for both of us.

Holding you both before God in his love,

Ailsa

THE WELL

Always it is there
at the bottom of the garden
of Everyman,
unobtrusive beyond the flowering shrubs,
cleverly concealed by the brambled growth,
the ominous well of despair.
To many it is given
never to see beyond the needing-weeding garden;
others must explore the piercing, well-surrounding
                                    thorns,
whilst some must uncover, discover
the fall.
All is given.

The shaft is bottomless;
hurtling
from life and from loves,
helpless
in the thickening, tumbling-down darkness,
the final foothold of hope – far-flung.

Where are you Lord?

Only trust echoes back,
Only trust is given;
God in hell,
Christ in the well
of the garden
of Everyman.

IT ISN'T EASY

It isn't easy being made,

submitting

to the melting down and hammering into shape,

feeling only the pain

without knowing the beauty.

Only stillness helps,

relaxing battered bodies and half-finished creations

into the sure hands of the Craftsman,

and trusting

that the chalice He has chosen to create

will prove fit for the wine of His presence.

My very dear Kate,

Thank you so much for writing and enclosing your poems. I was wondering why I hadn't heard from you for a while and am so sorry to learn how low you have been. You say you and Adam split up because you each wanted different things, and he, more of you than you could give, so that he even became possessive. It was such a courageous thing to break with him because I know you were very fond of him at one time, and however much you believe this to be the right move, it's bound to leave you with a sense of loss. There will be grief for the good things you shared and for the thought of what might have been. So try not to be hard on yourself, Kate, you are *allowed* to feel this way in the aftermath of a broken relationship.

I'm sure you're right that too much frenetic activity has also contributed to your depression and made you feel you're aching for stillness. So I'm glad the university doctor approves of your going off to Tymawr at the weekend. That is such good news. It's also good that you were able to identify the problem and do something to relieve it. You are a star! I know you will find time, space and loving at Tymawr, to help you rest, be still and renew. Dearest Kate, you are held in the palm of God's hand – and in my thoughts and prayers. 'At the turn of each tide He is there at my side and His touch is as gentle as silence.'

With all my love as always,

Ailsa

PS I enclose a poem written some time ago on Caldey Island* and look forward to yours from Tymawr!

Landscape is so different when the sun shines;
effortless then
the ancient, fresh-flower'd faces
of cliffs and community
celebrate the shimmering, incoming tide
of Your ocean of love.

---

* Home to a present-day community of Cistercian monks.

Yet in the darkness
the flowers still bloom
and through the night Vigil psalms rise,
ring'd round the island,
constant as the rocks on which they're built.

And you ask me to love You in the darkness,
to believe in Your smile
when I can no longer see Your face;
to love instead the secret of the night
and the sweet stillness of encounter –
'I am with you always to the end of time.'

Ascension Day – Caldey

'Come', you said, 'just as you are,
turn your face to Me whatever the weather
and through each season of your heart
bring Me the flowers that bloom along the way.'

And I come through daffodils and snow,
wounds still weeping
hurt not yet healed
trailing my brokenness to lay at Your feet.

Wounded hands reach out to receive,
with invitation to let go
and walk with You, hand-in-wounded-hand,
through the springtime of forgiveness.

Tymawr

Dearest Kate,

I was so glad to get your letter and quite wondrous poem, and recognise something of your old sparkle not too far under the surface.

What a lot of blessings! How wonderful that you felt drawn, almost physically, to return to Tymawr. I love your idea of 'running back to the everlasting arms'. And what a breakthrough that you now know you have to organise your life to allow time for silence and solitude. I am so pleased you are going to become an Associate of their community; that will give you a real sense of belonging.

So lovely that God gave you the *Poustinia* book to help you there. It's amazing how He inspired Catherine Doherty to recreate this Russian form of hermitage in the West. We need them today so much, these places for 'resting in the Lord' – as you have discovered. I was interested that the part of this book that chimed for you was the chapter where she speaks of the 'poustinia of the heart'. This seems very much to be the way God is leading you, Kate. It's the way we have spoken of before, where monasticism is interiorised, your heart is your cell, and the setting for contemplation is the marketplace.

You are right in saying that a certain amount of solitude is essential for those following this path. Actually, I would say, not only for them but for everyone. I'm not sure any mature personality can develop without time spent alone. Having said that, I feel it's important we don't try to create our own solitude. We need to keep listening as God speaks to us through the myriad little things of every day, and then allow Him to create it for us, along with the other good things He gives us, such as friends, family and study, all of which carry the message, 'Look how I love you!'

I do hope the sun will continue to come out from behind the clouds for you, Kate, and as you return to your studies you will remember those important words from the Tao of Pooh:

> *Don't underestimate the value of*
> *doing nothing, of just going along*
> *listening to all the things you can't hear*
> *and not bothering.*

You are always in my thoughts and prayers.

Love,

Ailsa

Dear Kate,

Greetings from Caldey! It has been a most beautiful week on all levels. Those of us staying at the guesthouse have been so lucky with the weather: wall-to-wall sunshine has blessed every day. All memories of previous visits with gale-force winds and driving rain are banished and there is a stillness about the island, especially in the early morning. Being on my own makes it a very different experience from the working visits – the times when I bring groups of people with mental health problems over for a few days' break.

It has been a time of gentle letting go, as well as receiving new treasures. I have been reminded of Anne Morrow Lindbergh's *Gift from the Sea*. She says: 'One cannot collect all the beautiful shells on the beach. One can collect only a few, and they are more beautiful if they are few.'

I am really writing now to share one of the treasures that I picked up this week. It's a little book, profound in its simplicity, called *Sleeping with Bread**. It could at first be mistaken for a children's book, but it offers a new and refreshing insight into the traditional Christian practice known as 'examination of conscience' ('examen'). This involved regularly acknowledging where (and how often!) we went wrong in God's sight. What *Sleeping with Bread** offers is a new and much more fruitful way of moving forward. (I'm quite excited about it, so forgive me if this turns out to be a long letter!)

The title of the book comes from a wartime practice of giving starving refugee children a piece of bread to hold at bedtime. So often they had not been able to sleep, from fear of waking up hungry and homeless again. Holding the bread was their guarantee that today they had eaten and tomorrow they would eat again. They could go safely to sleep in that security. An inspired idea, isn't it?

This symbol is picked up as an illustration of how a regular evening examen can work for us as a gentle looking back with God at the past day, to recognise His voice and His presence with us throughout all that happened, to see where and how we have responded to Him, and look trustfully forward to the next day. But instead

---

* Dennis, Sheila & Mathew Linn, Paulist Press (ISBN 0-8091-3579-5)

of asking ourselves the blunt question 'Where did I get things wrong?' the authors invite us to ask ourselves, in God's presence, two wonderfully simple questions about our experience of today:

For what moment today am I most grateful?
For what moment today am I least grateful?

We can word the questions in many other ways if we choose. (When was I happiest/saddest? What was today's high/low point? When did I feel God was nearest/furthest away?) If we make this a regular practice, over time we will begin to see patterns emerging, which will help us not just to understand ourselves better, but to know God better too. We'll become more sensitive to what truly brings us life, light and peace and what doesn't, and so be able to stay more continuously in that still centre you have begun to find. And if pain and sadness arise in us, we may discover unexpected blessings mysteriously linked with them – like your own experience of 'recognising God in the dark places as well as the light'.

This approach, by the way, relates to the 'consolation' and 'desolation' that figure so much in the spiritual masters, especially the sixteenth-century Spaniard, St Ignatius Loyola, whose teaching has been retrieved and found highly relevant for our times, whether for learning about prayer itself, or for helping to make decisions at turning points in our lives, such as your own right now, just about to finish at university.

So, my very dear Kate, I look forward to hearing news of where God will lead you and what 'sealed orders' lie in store for you. Meanwhile, I shall be ordering a copy of *Sleeping with Bread* for myself and I'll get one for you at the same time if you would like me to.

With my love and prayer always.

Please pray for me.

Ailsa

UNKNOWN COUNTRY

The way stretches ahead
from within this place
and moment of time,
wayless,
unformed,
with no light in its darkness.

And what else is there to do
when led through unknown country
at night
by a guide who goes his own way
keeping his thoughts to himself?
what else, but to put yourself in his hands.

Past all points of no return,
with no bird in the hand
should the two in your bush get away,
I stake my life on Your promise
and, taking Your hand,
plunge headlong into the all-embracing darkness.

Dearest Kate,

Wow! What a letter! And your poem 'Unknown Country' touched me very deeply, speaking more than volumes of prose about 'abandonment into God's hands'. It describes so well where you are at this point in your journey, as you leave the comparative security of a university campus for VSO in Africa. You are entering the unknown in all ways. I especially love the lines:

> *'with no bird in the hand*
> *should the two in your bush get away'*

That's absolutely you, Kate!

I don't know whether you will have read de Caussade's *Abandonment to Divine Providence*, but I assure you, you are living it. It's a book that can keep you company along the way and grow with you; whenever you return to it there will be new depths to be discovered – a little like a spiral staircase where over and over again you can look down on the same spot from another floor up. We are all asked to surrender ourselves to God but somehow we fear to push the boat out too far and put ourselves entirely in His hands. It's as if we can't really trust Him and are subconsciously wondering what He's going to do with us, thinking it must be something awful! And it's hard to give up control of our lives and allow the Holy Spirit to lead us – though I do believe that is exactly what you *are* doing right now, Kate. As you are learning, this is quite the reverse of a passive relinquishing of responsibility. Rather, it's having the courage to say 'yes' to life in all its fullness. If only we could see God's great love for us, longing to lead us to our heart's deepest desires! But we are so made that in this life we can only walk in faith and trust.

When we accept this 'All is harvest', as they say, and all things work together for our good, whether it seems like it or not. Keep travelling, dear Kate, and we will be in touch on the prayer-waves (as well as through Royal Mail!).

There is no path,
the path is made as we go;
pebbles carried
from the wild places of His love
with bruised hearts and bleeding fingers,
each one a given
fond – furthering our footsteps
and helping us home
to the waiting heart of the Father.

My love and prayers be with you, Kate. You are constantly in my heart.

Your ever-loving godmother,

Ailsa